Autism
Dad

Adventures in Raising An Autistic Son

D1293990

Essays by

Rob Errera

Cover design by Ed Gadomski

Autism Dad

CONTENTS

ACKNOWLEDGEMENTS

This book wouldn't be possible without the assistance of my editors at North Jersey Media Group, Nancy Rubenstein and Christa Limone. For the last twenty years they've given me a public forum to voice my opinions, a forum that gave rise to the essays in this book. Special thanks to eagle-eyed editor and heartfelt friend Ken Kimmel for his editorial advice and direction with this project and many others. I can't thank my wife and daughter enough - this book is their story, too. They inspire and nurture me every day. But this book is a gift to me from my son, one of many I've been blessed to receive.

For Rocco -- Buddies Forever

INTRO—THE BOOK THAT SHOULDN'T BE

I'm not supposed to write this book. I'm supposed to write science fiction and horror stories. That's what I've always wanted to do, what I've been doing since age seven. I'm supposed to be the next Stephen King.

But life had other plans for me, as it does for many of us. A long, strange trip led me to publishing this collection of essays, practically demanded it. I take the old adage, "write what you know" to heart. I write what I live.

There are nearly three million people in the United States who have autistic children, and countless more across the globe. Half of them are fathers,

Autism Dads, and chances are many of them have experienced—or will experience—some of the same things I have. This won't be a book of answers, or a how-to book. You won't find out how to recover your child from autism here (but you might elsewhere, so I encourage you to keep researching after you've finished reading this book).

I hope these essays show what it's like to live with and raise a child with autism. It's different than raising a typical child (I have one of those, too). The highs are higher, the lows are lower, and everything's more intense. At times this *is* a horror story (Note to Self: be careful what you wish for), but it's also a drama, a comedy, a political manifesto, a surreal farce, and a personal diary. Ultimately, it's a love story, as all good tales should be. Love is the engine that drives us all.

This is a book that should not be, yet already is. Most of these essays have already been published over the last eight years. I'm playing Dr. Frankenstein, sewing the pieces together, and waiting to see what rises from the slab.

PART I—DIAGNOSIS & BEYOND

I graduated from Rutgers University in New Jersey in the early 1990s with a journalism degree, and landed a job as a staff writer for the local weekly, The Wayne TODAY. The newspaper served the northern New Jersey communities of Wayne, Totowa, Little Falls, West Paterson, and others. The job taught me to meet tight deadlines and hone my writing chops. And, thanks to my editor, Nancy Rubenstein, I also got the opportunity to write my own opinion pieces twice a month. Thus, my bi-monthly column, *Hmm...* was born.

What does *Hmm...* mean? It's a sound of consideration, the sound you make when you're thinking deeply about a subject. Plus, I like that it's a word (and an ellipse) that can be pronounced with dozens of inflections to convey a variety of meanings, yet only when it's read does it encompass *all* of those meanings.

Hmm...

I got pretty good at writing columns, and won a bunch of awards from the regional journalism clubs. In 1996, I left the newspaper to take a job at a national magazine, but Nancy Rubenstein was kind enough to let me keep contributing two columns a month to Wayne TODAY.

Twenty years later I'm still hacking away, espousing my opinion, spreading my wisdom, and generally annoying the fine people of North Jersey. It's an awesome gig, because Nancy, and her successor at TODAY, Christa Limone, let me write about almost anything (as long as my topics and language stay suitable for a family newspaper—a challenge at times). Looking back over two decades of columns is like looking at snapshots of myself over the years. That's my life on those pages.

I've done a lot of living over the past twenty years. Milestones include getting married, getting divorced, getting remarried, and siring a son and a daughter. My wife and I were riding high and loving life when our son was born in January 2002. Check out this column and see how happy we were...silly fools!

GRADUATING FATHERHOOD BOOT CAMP
Reprinted from Wayne TODAY, March 2002

Six weeks of fatherhood, and already I'm defining myself by the way my kid sees me. I am Thick Hairy Arms that lift him up and down (which is different from Mom's Soft and Smooth Arms). I am Smiling Moon Face with Glasses at other times of the day. I am Stinky Breath at 4 a.m. Beard Stubble Man. I am Waiter, Maid, Chauffeur, Personal Assistant, and Wipe-My-Butt Guy.

Actually my wife is all of these things and more. I'm just the Assistant Waiter, Assistant Maid, etc. But in the past six weeks, I've gotten a good dose of fatherhood.

And I like it.

Like any new job, it's all fun and exciting right now. I'm sure there will be days ahead that won't be so much fun. But after completing six weeks, I'd say that fatherhood is shaping up to be one of the most interesting and rewarding jobs I've ever had. Like I said, it's early yet.

My son, Rocco (hey, no laughing at the name!) has taught me many things in only a short time. We already have a couple of things in common, big meals and long naps among them. Roc's not much for TV at this point, but he does enjoy watching the ceiling fan. Sometimes we'll watch it together for hours. Pretty lights...spinning things...*ooohhh... aaahhh...* Rocco has also helped me rediscover some of the little things that are easy to overlook in life. A warm blanket is good. A wet bottom is bad. A big dog licking your face is startling at first...but funny!

Rocco has taught me to appreciate sunrises, which I have seen more of in the last six weeks than in my entire 34 years prior. In fact, the whole sleep deprivation aspect of parenthood is something my wife and I severely underestimated. It's brutal. Over the past six weeks we've often wondered if our deceased relatives were aware of Rocco, watching over him like guardian angels. Thanks to the hallucinogenic properties of extreme sleep deprivation, our dead relatives actually drop in from time to time for a visit, if only to point and laugh.

The outpouring of generous gifts from well-wishers has pleasantly surprised Rocco and I. I'm also his Accountant and Asset Manager, heaven help the boy. That kid's getting gifts from all over, from people he's never even met! There's something about a newborn that gets people all excited, compels them to go to the mall and buy teddy bears and cute little outfits. I never quite understood what it was all about until now. Babies are good, one of the few truly good things life has to offer.

Most importantly, Rocco has taught me one of the great secrets of the universe. When I wake up in the middle of the night and ponder, "Why am I here? What is my purpose in life?", all I have to do is take a peek in his bassinet and go, "Oh. Yeah."

It's not that my life didn't have meaning and significance before my son was born. It's that everything up until now seems like practice.

I have seen the future, and it wears a onesie. And when I cradle tomorrow in my arms, it feels light as a feather.

+++++

Yes, the future wore a onesie, all powdery fresh and packed with potential. The next 18 months were some of the happiest of my life. In April 2003 my wife and I learned we were having another child and our joy increased tenfold. We were on a roll.

Then something went wrong. The futuristic onesie got all crapped up.

Shortly after his first birthday, Rocco started losing words. "Mama" and "Dada" went first, along with his eye contact. He stopped playing with toys. Instead he'd wander around aimlessly, opening and closing doors and drawers. A developmental pediatrician diagnosed Rocco with autism on August 13, 2003.

"He only seems moderately affected," the doctor said. "Not nearly as bad as some of the kids I've seen."

Maybe the doctor thought it was true, or maybe he told us what he thought we needed to hear. Either way, Laura and I were devastated. The drive home from the hospital that day was grim to say the least. My wife was in tears, I was enraged, and our 18-month-old son in the backseat was oblivious, and might remain so forever. One of the top developmental pediatricians in the state had just made our worst fears a reality.

"Call my OB-GYN when we get home," my wife said. She put her hand on her swollen belly. "No surprises. Find out the sex of this baby."

I knew what she was thinking. Autism is four times more prevalent in boys than girls. And if you have one autistic child, you have a 1-in-10 chance of having another. She was 22 weeks pregnant, but there was still time to terminate. We'd have to act fast, a couple of days, a week at most, but it could be done.

I shudder to think what would have happened if the doctor told us we were having another boy. We were both so hysterical, out of our minds.

It was a girl. Francesca Hope Errera arrived December 12, 2003, a ray of hope during an otherwise turbulent time. The fall of 2003 was exactly that -- a downward spiral for our family.

In September, a few weeks after our son's diagnosis, our beloved dog died, the giant mutt we adopted when we first moved in together. We half-joked that he was our first "first child," the start of our furry family. Now he was gone. And, in a way, our real first child had checked out, too. Our furry family was falling apart.

We were leveled, depressed, and overwhelmed. But there was no time to grieve. We contacted the state Early Intervention office, and Roc immediately began intensive Applied Behavior Analysis therapy. Each day it seemed we had another new ABA therapist in our home.

We tried to inform ourselves by reading every autism article we could find. We could rescue our son through diet and nutrition! Most of the dietary and biomedical interventions we tried *did* help our son, but none rescued him like we hoped.

I was afraid to write about my son's autism directly, as if writing about it would make it more real. It wasn't until nearly a year later when I finally took the plunge, and even then there's a strange, detached quality to this next column.

AUTISM AWARENESS HITS HOME
Reprinted from Wayne TODAY, July 2004

"Will you ever write a column about our son's autism?" my wife asks, not for the first time.

I've written all around it; I've written about removing milk from our son's diet, and I've written about the potential hazards of childhood vaccines. But I've never written about "It."

" I don't know," I tell her. "I don't know if I'm quite ready yet."

"It's been ten months since he was diagnosed," she gently prods. "I think you need to tell people."

"Tell people what?"

"About autism."

"What about it?" I say. "Where do I start?"

"Start with how it has changed our whole lives," she suggests. "Write about how it's consumed our lives, changed the way we do and think about everything."

Autism is a developmental disorder that affects a person's ability to communicate, process information, and understand emotions. When it begins, usually between 12-18 months of age, it's like your happy, loving child is abducted and replaced with a disinterested stranger. Autism doesn't end; there is no cure, though some kids, if they get proper treatment and are "responders," have found roads to recovery.

Rocco's autism diagnosis has changed everything for us. Nothing will ever be the same again. The future, once so bright and full of promise, has dark clouds on the horizon. Now it looks threatening and scary.

"Maybe," I say. "But I can't write about everything. I can't tell it all."

She knows what I'm talking about. The way your heart breaks every day, over and over again, a thousand times, even on a "good" day. How can I put that into words?

"No," she says. "You can't tell all of it. We need to keep some things private."

We have behavioral therapists from the state Early Intervention Services roaming through our house 20-plus hours each week. Privacy is another thing we've lost.

"I think it's important for people to hear about what an epidemic autism has become," my wife says. "It used to only happen to 1-in-10,000 kids. Now it's 1-in-150. Something's going wrong in our world. Something is triggering this. Something is damaging our children."

"Yeah, but nobody knows what it is," I tell her. "Is it vaccines? Food additives? Electro-magnetic waves? Mutated genetics? Better diagnostic criteria in childhood development? I don't want to lead anybody down the wrong path."

"But maybe you could help someone. These kids stand the best chance of getting better if they're diagnosed at a young age. Remember that woman we met at the park? Her son was almost three years old and still not talking before she got help. She kept her head in the sand for a long time. If people knew more about autism, they could get help earlier, when it's most helpful. Maybe you could help an autistic child if you wrote about it, Rob."

"Yes. Maybe I could."

"You could write about all the new kinds of treatments that are available for autistic kids. Not just the conventional stuff like behavioral therapy, but also the fringe stuff, like special diets and vitamin therapy. There's a whole biomedical approach to treating autism, things a mainstream doctor won't tell you. It might help if you wrote about it."

"Will it help our son? Will it help bring him back?"

This is the question we've been asking for nearly a year. She doesn't know the answer any more than I do, but we keep asking it anyway. Rocco has made improvements, but a "big breakthrough" continues to elude us. We keep trying.

"I don't know," she says. "But it might help *you*."

She's smart, my wife. She knows that writing is more than something I do for fun and (very little) profit. It's how I work out problems. It's where I tell the truth. It's how I cope.

"Maybe you're right," I say, already knowing she is. "But it's still too hard. I don't think I'm ready yet. But soon..."

+++++

Response to the previous column was underwhelming to say the least.

There was none.

That's another strange thing about writing a newspaper column: people sometimes don't react to my work the way I expect. I'll write what I think is an innocuous piece about cable television rates, school busing policies, or some funny thing that happened to me at the supermarket, and I'll get all kinds of reader response. But if I spill my heart and soul out for 1,000 words I get squat. Ah well, such is the nature of pearls before swine. Or maybe I just stink at critiquing my own stuff.

I shied away from writing about autism again for another six months. Maybe I did write about it again in 2004—I honestly don't remember. The entire year was such a bleak blur, punctuated by a couple of computer mishaps that wiped out a lot of data (writing, as well as most of my daughter's baby photos).

What my wife and I *did* do that year was spend a lot of money trying to help our son, way more money than we had. We tried as many different therapies as we could, some traditional, some completely unconventional. This was a trend that continued for years, until we ran out of money, until we dug a hole so deep, we had to borrow money just to pay the minimums on our outstanding loans. We remain there, on the brink of financial collapse, to this day.

This isn't a book about dietary or biomedical interventions for autism. I told you upfront this isn't a how-to-cure-autism book. I'd give anything to write that book. But I was meant to write this one instead.

What are biomedical interventions for autism? It's giving your kid various vitamins and supplements in an effort to realign his or her body chemistry. Many autistic people are deficient in B-vitamins, among other things. Adding vitamins, either through diet or nutritional supplements, can help improve cognitive function in autistic children (or any child, for that matter).

There are plenty of books discrediting biomedical treatments for autism, chief among them Paul Offit's self-serving shit-fest, *Autism's False Prophets*. I have to hand it to Offit, he did come up with a great title. There are many false prophets in the newfound cottage industry of autism treatment. Plenty of charlatans, quacks, and snake oil salesmen, too.

But there are also many fine doctors (and teachers, therapists, etc.) who are diligently working to find root causes and legitimate treatments for autism. Some are specialists, working their own individual part of the puzzle. Others try to fit existing pieces together. I imagine these doctors working together over a massive table, trying to fit the various pieces of the autism jigsaw puzzle together. And Paul Offit's standing over their shoulders, busting his colleagues' balls when they put a piece in wrong, and discouraging others from coming to the table and contributing to the puzzle's solution. Dickhead.

There are many books espousing new and improved ways to recover your child from autism. I'd recommend Christie Burnett's account *Finding Anthony*. Anthony Burnett was Rocco's kindergarten classmate. Thanks to a combination of biomedical treatments (MB-12 shots and others) and Verbal Behavior therapy, Anthony is now mainstreamed in a public elementary school. I believe recovery is possible (and vast improvements are probable) with proper diet and supplementation. I've seen it happen with Anthony Burnett.

But not every treatment works for every child. Rather, each kid requires an individual treatment plan. Even then, there's a chance you may never find a treatment that helps your kid. But how will you know unless you try? And, as a parent, shouldn't you try to do everything possible to give your child the greatest chance at success?

When my wife and I fight (more often in the early days, less frequently now) one of her killer jabs is, "It's all about money with you!"

This never fails to push my buttons. The comment implies that money is more important to me than treating my son's autism, and that is *not* true! But I'd be lying if I said money isn't a factor in his treatment. Autism specialists are expensive (around $400 an hour), and I've only met a couple over the years (one, actually) who offered discounts and *pro bono* treatments for autistic kids. My wife's jab is a killer because there's a hint of truth to it.

I won't defend our son's autism treatments (or the financial repercussions thereof). Laura and I did what we did, spent what we spent, and would do most of it all over again if we had to. We had to *know*, and, frankly, it's only money. No regrets, only some remorse the various treatments we tried with Rocco weren't more successful. As my wife likes to point out, Rocco might be in *worse* shape if we hadn't tried all the treatments we did. Still you can feel my financial pain in the column below.

FEELING ILL OVER HEALTH INSURANCE
Reprinted from Wayne TODAY, January 2005

If you're like most Americans, one of the main reasons you have a job is to get health insurance through your employer. For some, having health insurance is even more important than the paycheck itself. The problem is sometimes when you really *need* health insurance, it's nowhere to be found, even if you've been paying for years.

Example 1: My father. For 40 years he worked hard, duly paying his health insurance premiums. When, at the age of 61, he was asked to accept an early retirement package, he took it. Why not head down to Florida a few years early and enjoy the new dream home? He and Mom only had to stay healthy for a couple of years before they got health coverage through Medicare.

But the following year my Dad was diagnosed with cancer. He looked around for coverage, but the health insurance companies wanted nothing to do with him and his "preexisting medical condition." He was on his own.

As my father pursued various cancer treatments, he was surprised to find many of the doctors he visited were accustomed to dealing with uninsured patients.

"We have two price lists," one nurse told him. "One for people with health insurance, and one for people without." In many cases, the un-insured price was less than half. One company charged nearly $3,000 for an MRI scan billed through insurance, but only charged my father a little over $1,000. It's no wonder insurance premiums are so high.

My father saw good doctors and tried several types of treatments, but nothing worked. He died a little over two years after he was diagnosed. I don't know if having health insurance would have changed the way doctors treated Dad's cancer. But I'm sure it would have left my Mom with more money in the bank.

Example 2: Me. For nearly 20 years I've been working and paying for health insurance. Now that I have a couple of young kids, I need health insurance more than ever. What if something terrible should happen?

Well, in August 2003 something terrible *did* happen—my son was diagnosed with autism, a neurological disorder that affects each child differently. Covering the expenses associated with treating autism is a gray area in the eyes of insurers. Since much of the treatment is based on behavior modification therapy, many health insurance companies believe the bills should be paid by local school districts. It's an educational expense, right? But many school districts believe health insurance companies should foot the bill. After all, autism is a medical condition, no? As a result, the people most often stuck with the bill are the parents.

I should be happy that I live in New Jersey, where much of the behavioral therapy is covered by the state's Early Intervention program. New Jersey is also one of only six states that require health insurers to cover autism-related expenses. But getting insurance companies to cover the cost of treating autism medically is a struggle. I know several families with autistic kids who have taken out home equity loans and/or second mortgages to pay for their children's medical treatments. I've paid a lot of my son's medical bills with credit cards...now I'm refinancing my home for the third time in order to pay back Citibank. Over the past year I've submitted over $5,000 in medical claims to my insurance company. So far they've only reimbursed us $227.

The purpose of this column isn't to complain about my financial woes (but thank you for listening). The point is that a message needs to be sent to insurance companies *and* medical providers *and* educators about autism expenses. Other disabilities—like CP or MS—are clearly recognized and covered by most insurers, yet autism—maybe because it doesn't *look* like anything—remains poorly understood and even more poorly compensated.

Football great Dan Marino, whose son is autistic, formed the Dan Marino Foundation in 1992 with the purpose of lobbying insurance companies to cover autism-related expenses. Dan Marino earned a good living as a professional athlete, and is probably one of the few people who can afford the best therapeutic and medical treatments for his son.

But he understands the financial demands of having an autistic child. It's bad enough that the parents of autistic children have to bear such heartache in life—they shouldn't be left penniless, too.

+++++

There's a reason the symbol for autism awareness is a puzzle piece. It's a truly mysterious disorder. What causes it? How do you treat it? Why do autistic kids behave so strangely? Why are so many kids being diagnosed as autistic these days? So many questions, too few answers.

The mystery my wife and I were trying to solve in 2005 was, "What happened to our son? Where did he go, and how do we get him back?" It really *was* like a kidnapping. Where had our son gone? Who was this strange kid, who *looked* like our son, but mostly ignored us in favor of repeatedly opening and closing doors, watching faucets run, and eating liquid soap? What ransom needed to get paid in order to get him back?

My wife always felt there was a giant clock hanging over Rocco's head, a countdown on the limited window of time we had to help him. We needed to recover Roc by the time he was three years old...five...seven...nine. The clock kept ticking, the years rolled by, and we weren't any closer to our goal of recovering our son. Each sweep of the minute hand brought us closer to the realization he may *never* recover.

It was a stressful, anxious time for both of us. We were doing everything we could for our son, and nothing was working. At least it wasn't working the way *we* wanted it to.

Eventually we stopped looking at the imaginary clock hanging over our son's head (well, I still glance at it from time to time, and see frightening milestones like puberty, adolescence, and adulthood up ahead) and allowed things to unfold at their own pace. Don't swim against the tide. Go with the flow.

This next column was published nearly two years after our son's diagnosis. I was getting a clearer picture of what it meant to be Autism Dad.

TOP FIVE WAYS AUTISM CHANGES YOUR LIFE
Reprinted from Wayne TODAY, July 2005

Autism is a pervasive developmental disorder that affects 1-in-150 children. My son is one of them. Rocco was diagnosed with autism nearly two years ago at the age of 18-months, and we struggle every day with the communication and processing challenges that autism presents.

Some days I think autism is contagious (it's not) because it has a way of permeating every part of your life, coloring every aspect of everything you do, and can make you live in an insular world of your own. Autism changes not only your child's life forever, but also the lives of everyone who loves and cares about you and your child. Autism has a way of spreading in unseen and unexpected ways. Below are five ways autism has changed life for my family.

1) **Financial**—If you want to treat autism aggressively, like we have, it's going to cost a lot of money. Probably more than you have, even if you consider yourself "wealthy" (we never did, and now we definitely aren't). Very few biomedical treatments for autism are covered by health insurance. Private therapy is also costly, and often ends up being an out-of-pocket expense.

2) **Time**—Raising a young child takes a lot of time. Raising an autistic child takes ten times the amount of work. If you want your child to get better, you need to engage him every waking moment of the day. There's no plopping your kid down in front of

the TV—if you want your kid to live in this world, you have to constantly draw him out of his.

3) **Exhaustion**—The effort it takes to help your child recover from autism is enormous. Maintaining a special diet, preparing for doctors' appointments, and organizing therapy schedules are just a few of the chores added to the already hectic job of childrearing. Personal hobbies and interests fall by the wayside; you're too tired to do much of anything, even if you had the time or money.

4) **Relationships**—In times of crisis you find out who your true friends are. We've lost a few friends since our son's diagnosis. We've gained a few new ones, too (and then lost a couple of them!). The same goes for family members; some have stepped up to offer help and support, others faded into the background. Having an autistic child can make you self-absorbed, irritable, depressed, and emotionally unstable, all of which put a strain on personal relationships. It takes a heavy toll on a marriage, too; it's estimated that 80 percent of parents of autistic children get divorced or separated. My wife and I lean on each other heavily—so much so, that sometimes I fear we will crush each other. Autism has a way of revealing whether or not you've chosen your spouse wisely; my wife and I are both pleased with the choices we made.

5) **The Future**—When a baby is born, parents have high hopes their child will rise above the pack, and have a lifetime of achievement. When your child is diagnosed with autism, you suddenly strive to have your child "indistinguishable from his peers." Just being "normal" would be a major accomplishment. Instead of looking at your toddler and wondering what college he will go to, you wonder if he'll ever be able to live on his own, and what will happen to your child after you die.

The above examples are not presented as a cry for sympathy ("There goes that guy from the TODAY paper, griping about his personal life again...") I present them because autism is an epidemic.

With 1-in-150 kids diagnosed with autism, there are a lot of families out there affected by this disorder. Maybe you know someone who has an autistic child. (If not, I fear you soon will.) Chances are they've experienced one or more of the aforementioned life-changes. With the exception of a few rare childhood illnesses, autism is one of the most labor-intensive disabilities to contend with. And, unlike some tragic childhood ailments, you don't know how your child's story is going to turn out.

Given the right combination of treatments, some children make a full recovery from autism. Others are classic "non-responders." But there are new therapies being developed every day, and even autistic adults, whom many consider "too far gone," are benefiting from these emerging treatments.

As the parent of an autistic child, you never stop searching, never stop trying, and never stop hoping for a way to help your child. It's an everyday struggle, a lifelong battle that parents of young children are being asked to face. Offer them whatever help you can; even a kind word makes a difference.

+++++

You see me cracking, right? "Even a kind word makes a difference"? Can you say, "cry for help"?

I was drowning (so was my wife) and the stress of the holidays didn't help...but it did open my eyes to the importance of our support network.

HAPPY HARRIED HOLIDAYS
Reprinted from Wayne TODAY, December 2005

Last year my holiday column was about how efficient I was, how my house was decorated, the cards were sent, and all my shopping was done two weeks before Christmas. I was going to have time to enjoy the holidays for a change.

This year I'm back to "normal," which for me means two weeks behind. Christmas is days away and I haven't bought one present. I hung some twinkling lights outside the house after Thanksgiving, and erected our cheesy three-foot plastic tree (much to my wife's chagrin; her hatred for this tree grows with each passing year). I haven't found time to do much else in the way of decorating.

Nowhere is our holiday chaos better exemplified than in our family photo. Our first photo session was the day after Thanksgiving. The plan was to shoot the kids standing by the Christmas tree, looking cute. Francesca wanted no part of it; she threw herself on the floor, kicking and screaming. It was two weeks before her second birthday, but she was already deep into the terrible twos. Things got out of hand and the tree toppled. We got one good photo of the tree falling over, and the kids screaming in terror.

We tried again a few days later. This time Rocco was the problem. He didn't want to stand next to his sister. He pitched a fit. His eyes got red and puffy from crying. He looked like Tiny Tim in all the pictures.

We tried again and again throughout the week, in all sorts of settings, from jumping on our bed to splashing in the tub. Nothing was suitable for a holiday photo. To make matters worse, we were starting to get cards from friends and family, all with pictures of their happy, smiley, well-behaved children. We got discouraged. We were *never* going to get a nice holiday photo of our kids.

Part of the problem was that we set the bar high. Our Christmas photo last year was *really* cute, and we felt we had to at least match that. We were surprised and flattered several times during the past year when we'd visit the homes of people we knew, and find our kids' Christmas photo still taped to their fridge, even in the middle of July. Our kids really *did* look cute!

Another problem was the importance my wife and I placed on our holiday photo. We struggle daily with the challenges presented by Rocco's autism. It affects every member of our family, every day, in every way. Our life is far from normal, yet we want our kids to appear that way, at least for a brief moment, once a year. We're so proud of them both; we just want them to look as beautiful as we think they are.

We caught a break after a recent snowfall. We took the kids outside and perched them atop our slide. I jumped up and down, blowing bubbles and singing songs as my wife snapped away. Nobody called the cops, and we got a decent shot—Rocco is smiling uncertainly, and Francesca has her mouth open like she's about to laugh or vomit. It's not as good as last year's holiday photo, but it will do.

I made a late-night run to the 24-hour CVS to use their holiday photo card machine. There was a mom ahead of me trying to print out a holiday photo of her kids—two little girls who looked like they had just finished a heated wrestling match. I was secretly pleased to see that our photo looked slightly less chaotic. I was also glad to see I wasn't the only parent who waited until the last minute to send their Christmas cards out.

I was helping my wife stuff the cards into envelopes the next day, when she reiterated her belief that our holiday photo wasn't as good as last year's.

"We probably won't see it hanging in people's homes this year," she said.

"I don't know about that," I said. "I don't think people kept our Christmas card around because our kids are so cute, or because we're such a great photography team. I think it's because our family is always in their thoughts and prayers."

Suddenly our two-foot stack of holiday cards took on a new meaning.

So that's the holiday lesson I learned this year. It's not so much about decorating the tree, or buying gifts, or how you look in your holiday photo. It's about acknowledging the people who love and support you throughout the year. Sometimes you don't have to look any further than your Christmas card list.

ENDNOTE: Our holiday photo sessions have gotten easier as our children got older. But mostly we stopped putting so much pressure on getting the "perfect photo." If you can't change a situation, change the way you react to it.

PART II—AUTISM, VACCINES & THE MEDIA

What's one of the most annoying things about being the parent of an autistic child? The public meltdowns? The repetitive behaviors? The communication problems?

There are two extremely annoying things about being Autism Dad. I'll tell you about the worst thing later. But the other is reading reports about autism in the mainstream media.

For the most part, the stuff I read and see on TV are recycled press releases from the Centers for Disease Control. Not much investigative reporting going on, just a bunch of lazy "journalists" parroting back what a government agency wants them to. I don't want to sound like a conspiracy nut, but it makes me suspicious. These aren't cub reporters taking the easy way out; these are esteemed talking heads like Matt Lauer dropping the ball.

In order to treat a disease, you have to know its cause, but nobody knows exactly what causes autism, or why autism rates are rising. Is it linked to childhood vaccines?

I don't know. As the following columns show, I used to firmly believe childhood vaccines caused my son's autism. Now, I'm not so sure. Study after study show there's no proven link between autism and vaccines. (Although, the studies show there's no proven link between autism and the mumps/measles/rubella vaccine [the MMR shot], they don't look at a possible link between autism and *all* childhood vaccines combined.)

Even if you can't cure a disease, science is usually able to pinpoint a cause. We know what causes cancer, Alzheimer's, and AIDS, and subsequently, we're getting better at treating those diseases.

Why can't science find a cause for the autism epidemic? Plenty of money is being put into research. Can't science come up with something better than, "there's a genetic component"? We knew that 40 years ago, and genetics don't explain the sudden rise in autism rates—the human gene pool doesn't change that rapidly. There's got to be an environmental trigger. If it's not childhood vaccines, what is it?

The lack of answers is not only frustrating, it's suspicious, like someone is deliberately pocketing pieces of the autism puzzle.

AUTISM EPIDEMIC—CDC KEEPS HEAD IN THE SAND
Reprinted from Wayne TODAY, March 2007

First it was 1-in-10,000. Then it was 1-in-5,000. Then 1-in-1,000. Now, according to a new study released by the Centers for Disease Control, the rate of autism in this country is 1-in-150. And, in our neck of the woods of Northern New Jersey, those numbers are less than 1-in-100. Young boys in New Jersey have a 1-in-60 chance of being autistic.

My son is one of those children.

Yet, despite these statistics, the CDC refuses to admit that the number of autistic children is on the rise. They deny an epidemic their own studies confirm time and time again.

The CDC believes the number of autistic kids is rising because of better diagnostic tools. Kids that were once labeled mentally retarded, slow, badly behaved, or even "painfully shy" are now falling under the umbrella of autism. Indeed, autism is a spectrum disorder, which means some are severely affected, and others only mildly so.

But maybe the CDC's definition of autism is too broad. The diagnostic tools are not "better" if more and more children are being labeled with a lifelong disability. Maybe autism needs to be broken down into further classification—Type I, Type II, etc.

But whatever name you give it, the fact remains that 1-in-150 American children are suffering from severe learning disabilities. That's a problem of epidemic proportions—a problem that simply wasn't there 25 years ago.

And the CDC refuses to acknowledge it.

The hope following the CDC's report is that more money will be spent on autism research. Since the report was released, New Jersey legislators have already pushed through a bill increasing autism research grants by $4 million.

The money is desperately needed. The cause of autism is unknown. There is a genetic component to autism, but that wouldn't explain the sharp increase in rates; there has to be some environmental trigger that's causing the number of autistic children to rise so dramatically.

At the risk of sounding like a nutty conspiracy theorist, I don't think the CDC really *wants* to find the root cause of the autism epidemic. Then somebody would be held accountable. Someone would be liable. If not the pharmaceutical companies who make harmful vaccines, then the FDA, which approves them, or the pediatricians who over-prescribe them, or maybe the corporate giants that pollute the environment.

Why is the autism rate in New Jersey so high? My wife thinks it's because New Jersey has a good Early Intervention system, and parents with autistic children are moving to New Jersey to take advantage of the state's services. Scan the autism message boards on the Web, and you'll find dozens of parents of autistic children looking to relocate to New Jersey. There are more and more of them each week.

But I think the high autism rate in New Jersey has to do with the toxic nature of the Garden State. New Jersey has 108 toxic waste dumps, the most of any state in the nation. New Jersey is also the largest chemical-producing state in the nation. New Jersey has the largest petroleum containment area outside of the Middle East. New Jersey is also rife with naturally occurring health hazards, like radon gas. Any or all of these factors could be the environmental trigger(s) that lead to autism. That's where I'd like to see research dollars spent.

The staggering number of autistic children is a sign something has gone very, very wrong in our world. Something is stealing a significant portion of our children away from us. The CDC needs to stop its charade ("There aren't more autistic kids today than 25 years ago...we're *counting* them better") and start asking *why*.

I don't want to find the cause for the autism epidemic because I want to sue somebody. I want to find the cause because that's how you find a cure. Like any parent of an autistic child, I want to find a way – *any* way – to help my kid get better.

LEGAL BATTLE COULD END AUTISM'S CIVIL WAR
Reprinted from Wayne TODAY, June 2007

There's a civil war going on in the world of autism. But there's a big battle underway that may settle the score once and for all.

Autism Speaks is a charity organization founded by former NBC chairman Bob Wright and his wife Suzanne in 2004 after their grandson, Christian, was diagnosed with the disorder. In a few short years, Autism Speaks has become one of the biggest and most influential autism charities, thanks in part to the Wrights' celebrity friends (Jerry Seinfeld and Paul Simon) and the couple's connections with media outlets.

But in the last few years, the Wrights have had a severe falling-out with their daughter Katie, Christian's mother, over the cause of their grandson's autism. Katie Wright believes her son's autism was caused by vaccine damage. Her son, like mine and many other autistic children, regressed into an autistic state following his MMR vaccine. Katie Wright has spoken out about vaccines and other possible environmental causes of autism on "Oprah," and has appeared in interviews alongside controversial author David Kirby. Kirby's book, *Evidence of Harm*, examines not only the link between autism and exposure to mercury preservatives in vaccines, but also the political and financial influence of vaccine-makers who wish to suppress this information.

Bob and Suzanne Wright quickly issued a press release stating, "Katie Wright is not a spokesperson for Autism Speaks." The Wrights don't want to be drawn into the autism-vaccine debate. Why not? Because the big pharmaceutical companies that manufacture vaccines are the same ones who fund all the major media outlets. Commercials for prescription drugs pay the bills at ABC, CBS, NBC, etc. The ties between media outlets and drug companies run long and deep; remember Geritol's involvement with the rigged game show "21" back in the 1950s? Check out the movie *Quiz Show* if you don't.

But a trial underway in federal claims court may finally put the issue of an autism-vaccine link to rest. The "Vaccine Court" is a division of the U.S. Court of Federal Claims set up to hear cases about vaccine damage. The court is finally ruling on the nearly 5,000 claims filed by parents of autistic children. If the court agrees there is a link between autism and vaccines, parents may be awarded compensation from a special government trust fund. As of this writing, the court case is just beginning. Both sides are presenting scientifically backed studies, both sides have experts looking to discredit the other's science and research methods.

I believe the parents have a good shot at winning this one. For starters, they only have to prove that a link between autism and immunization shots is more likely than not, based on a preponderance of evidence. And if there's ever a place where guilt can be "safely" admitted in the autism epidemic, then the Vaccine Court is it. The federal trust fund is financed by a 75 cents-per-vaccine tax paid by consumers, so it won't cost the vaccine-manufacturers a penny, and they can never be held liable for any damage caused by their vaccines. It's kind of like O.J. Simpson being found innocent in criminal court, but guilty in civil court. The vaccine manufacturers, and the medical community that endorses their products, will get away with a crime, but some money may be awarded to cover the damages.

The hope here is that this trial will result in a change in the immunization schedule endorsed by the American Academy of Pediatrics. Slow down. Spread vaccines out. Don't give so many all at once, and at such a young age. Abolish a blanket immunization policy—every child must have Vaccine A at 3 months, Vaccine B at 6 months, Vaccine C at 12 months—but tailor it to suit each individual child. Only give them a vaccine when they're healthy enough to accept it, and wait a while before giving them another.

Some argue that altering the vaccine schedule will unnecessarily expose children to the risk of infectious disease. But why would anyone fear a possible outbreak of mumps, measles or whooping cough when a real outbreak of autistic spectrum disorders, a lifelong developmental disability, is currently raging?

If there's even a hint that vaccines might be a trigger for autism—and I believe there's more than a hint—then the medical community, drug makers, and government regulators need to take a step back and reexamine this issue more closely. With any luck that's what the Vaccine Court will find.

Then, maybe, the Wrights can put their family feud to rest.

ENDNOTE: The Federal Vaccine Court did not side with the parents of autistic children, further discrediting a link between childhood vaccines and autism. I don't know if Katie Wright ever reconciled with her parents. The environmental triggers of autism—if any—remain a mystery.

LIKE STIMS THROUGH THE HOURGLASS...SOAPS TACKLE THE DRAMA OF AUTISM
Reprinted from Wayne TODAY, October 2008

There's trouble in Salem. Elvis Junior has impregnated two women. Neither is his wife, and one just entered the witness protection program. Kate is dying of cancer, yet still finds time to make out with her hunky doctor. And somebody stuck a knife in Trent Robbins' back, killing him. Who did it? His own daughter, Melanie, whom he pimped out to pay off gambling debts? Her brother, Max? Grand dame Caroline, who was found kneeling over Trent's body holding a bloody knife? His secret wife, Nicole? (Yeah, they're married but nobody knows...*shhh*!)

Like sands through the hourglass, so are the *Days of Our Lives*. NBC's popular daytime soap opera has been running for over forty years—and the plot lines keep getting more twisted. It's the only soap my wife watches (or so she claims) and now—because I'm a wonderful husband who shares his wife's interests—I kinda watch it, too. Like any soap opera, *Days of Our Lives* (DOOL in soap speak) is ridiculous, outlandish and chock full of over-the-top melodrama. It's the last place you'd expect to see a "realistic" storyline.

So when two characters on the show, Abe and Lexi Carver, recently had their toddler son, Theo, diagnosed with autism, my wife and I were skeptical about how the show would handle the storyline. Our son has autism, so we're intimately familiar with the challenges of raising a special-needs child. There are times when our real lives make soap opera shenanigans look like child's play.

"You watch," I told my wife. "Now that their kid has autism, you'll never see him on the show again. He might show up again in six months...and he'll be a typical teenager heading off to college."

This is a standard soap opera technique. Characters have babies yet you rarely see them *raising* their kids. That takes place off-screen someplace. And soap opera kids have a way of aging quickly; an infant can become a toddler literally overnight, and show up a few weeks later as a "tween." It's not uncommon for a soap opera baby to vanish, only to reappear a few years later as a "promiscuous teen" played by some hot, young actor or actress willing to don skimpy outfits. That's the soap opera way.

So we were surprised when *Days* chose to inject some reality into its autism storyline. Theo's autism diagnosis has shaken Lexi and Abe's marriage to its core. Neither one can think of anything but their son. Lexi has a breakdown in the park as she watches Theo stim and typical kids play. ("Stim" is short for "self stimulatory behavior" like spinning, hand flapping, or any bizarre, repetitive behavior. If your kid is autistic, your kid stims.)

There's a corny "Gift of the Magi" moment when Lexi realizes she has to step down from her job as chief of staff at the hospital to spend more time with her son. She goes home and finds that Abe has quit his job as chief of police so that he can do the same. Corny, yes, but there's a kernel of truth, too. When your kid is diagnosed with autism, at least one parent is going to have to give up the career they studied, trained and worked to get, and take up a new career as "autism expert" for their kid. That's the way it has to be. A couple of weeks ago, Lexi and Abe spent a few panicked days after Theo wandered off. Autistic kids are a flight risk; it's a real concern of any parent with an autistic child.

It turns out *Day of Our Lives* writer Dena Higley has a son with autism, and knows very well how it impacts the lives of real parents. Higley's son was a non-verbal, stimmy toddler prone to behavioral outbursts. But years of intensive therapy paid off for the Higleys. Though her son, Connor, is still on the autistic spectrum, his symptoms have subsided, and now he's in his sophomore year at college.

"We never used autism as a way of making excuses or setting boundaries," Higley explains. "Connor never let autism define who he was."

That's the message she hopes to pass on to the viewers of *Days of Our Lives*, many of whom are young mothers. Higley wants to realistically portray the challenges of raising an autistic child, but also offer hope and progress to those with special-needs kids.

Still, my wife and I find that DOOL is not 100-percent accurate. Lexi still finds time to wear fancy clothes and make-up every day, something the average "autism mom" rarely has time for. And though Abe's put his career as a detective on hold, he's running for mayor of Salem. (The current mayor was assassinated, so it might not be much of a race...and so are the *Days of Our Lives*.)

DOOL is far from the first daytime drama to address real social issues. In 1983, *All My Children* broke ground by introducing one of daytime's first openly gay characters. An interracial couple got married onscreen on *General Hospital* in 1987, and an AIDS patient had a romantic storyline on *AMC* in the late '80s.

But Higley's DOOL storyline is the first to show the challenges of autism realistically in a daytime drama. And, with autism rates at an all-time high and rising, now is the right time. I hope Higley is able to keep her storyline real. You don't have to look far for drama when your kid has autism—there are heartaches and miracles happening every day.

That's something mothers of autistic children should see. Maybe they need to see that they can still be beautiful and vivacious like Lexi. The passion they display for their children imbues them with a beauty far deeper than the clothes they wear, or the way they style their hair.

Now, if they would only bring Jack back...

WHY DOES MATT LAUER SUCK?
Reprinted from Wayne TODAY, September 2009

Matt Lauer is a cheese-ball.

The latest proof of his journalistic cheesiness was the *Dateline NBC* special aired last week entitled "A Dose Of Controversy." It was supposed to be an in-depth look at the possible link between childhood vaccines and autism, with Matt Lauer promising "common sense" advice for parents of young children.

Instead the *Dateline* report focused on one vaccine, the MMR shot, and Dr. Andrew Wakefield, a British scientist who published a study questioning the safety of the MMR vaccine back in 1998. Wakefield's nemesis is Paul Offit, head of infectious disease at Children's Hospital in Philadelphia and author of the book *Autism's False Prophets*, who claims Wakefield is spreading false science. Offit blames Wakefield for the falling vaccination rates in the UK and the United States. Both sides point fingers.

So what's the common sense advice for parents? Incredibly, Matt Lauer closes his piece by reading a press release from the American Academy of Pediatrics urging parents to vaccinate their children according to their advised schedule.

Reading from a press release, Matt? Is this what passes for investigative journalism these days? *Cheese-ball*!

As the parent of an autistic kid this type of "news" coverage infuriates me. I won't lie to you—I *do* think vaccines played a role in my son's autism. Maybe it wasn't the mercury in the shots (my son was at the tail end of the thimerosol shots) and maybe it wasn't the MMR vaccine (though my son was never "right" again after he got his) but maybe it was a combination of the 26 shots he received before he was 18 months old. My son was a tiny baby, born a couple of weeks early. Common sense tells you those are a lot of shots for a tiny immune system to process.

Why so many shots? Good question. Matt Lauer should ask it. When my wife and I were new parents, we went to a pediatrician who followed the guidelines of the American Academy of Pediatrics to the letter. We did what Matt Lauer would have told us to do.

And when our son was diagnosed with autism at 18 months old, we did what Paul Offit would have told us to do; we relied on the resources of conventional medicine.

And frankly, those resources sucked.

The developmental pediatrician who diagnosed our son handed us a bunch of old pamphlets that told us autism is incurable, and that 80-percent of autistic kids are retarded. We started working our way through the maze of Early Intervention services (militant-style behavior therapy with a mixed bag of therapists) and our school system. It wasn't long before we realized that mainstream treatments for autism were weak; not enough hours, not enough trained therapists, not enough anything.

Your pediatrician will happily write your child a prescription for Ritalin or Risperidone, however.

Whether you agree with Andrew Wakefield's theories or not, there are certain undeniable truths about this new generation of autistic kids. Get any ten of them in a room and eight will have some type of digestive problem: diarrhea, constipation, limited diet, etc. And once you start treating those "gut problems" many of these kids start getting better.

That's fact. That's news. That's the real story.

But you almost never see that story in the mainstream media. You don't see big government-funded studies looking into the "gut-brain connection." You don't see reporters digging to find out what new autism treatments are working. Instead you get more "studies" declaring vaccines safe. You get Matt Lauer reading a press release. It makes me want to throw things at my television set.

Because autism is a treatable disease, maybe even a curable one. Yes, the biomedical treatment of autism is a field rife with charlatans, the "false prophets" of Paul Offit's book. (I could fill a book of my own with all of the snake oil salesmen my wife and I have encountered over the years.) But there are also a lot of good people—good doctors, good therapists, good scientists—out there developing valid new treatments for autistic kids. Not every treatment works for every child, but some do.

That's where doctors, scientists and journalists should focus their energies. Explore these new treatments, sift out the "false prophets" from the "real deals," find out what's working and—more importantly—*why* it's working. Instead of trying to revoke Andrew Wakefield's medical license, why not take a look at the research he and his colleagues are doing, and see what they've found?

Instead of funding another "vaccines and autism" study, maybe the government should fund a study where 1,000 autistic kids get free meythl-B12 shots for a year. I'd bet that 60-80 percent of those kids would show improvements in language and social skills at the end of that study.

Maybe *Dateline NBC* and Matt Lauer should follow 10 autistic children as they start on a gluten-free, casein-free diet and track their improvements, if any. Give the caregivers of autistic children some tangible information they can work with, not rhetoric and press releases.

Want some common sense advice on vaccinating your baby? Here it is:

Space the shots out.

The vaccination timetable set by the American Academy of Pediatrics is like every other public health policy—it's tailored to cover the lowest common denominator, the babies most at risk for diseases like hepatitis and diphtheria. If your baby lives in a tenement, or is tossed into a germy daycare environment at six weeks old, then maybe you'd feel safer following the AAP's shot schedule.

But if your baby is like many babies and pretty much sticks close to home for the first couple years of its life, then they probably don't need all the shots the AAP recommends as early as they recommend them. I'm sure a pediatrician will write in to tell you differently. But common sense should tell you otherwise.

Matt Lauer should have too.

BREAKING NEWS: GAME OVER, AUTISM WINS
Reprinted from Wayne TODAY, February 2010

Have you heard the news? Turns out that whole vaccine/autism debate was all made up by one doctor in England; he was found guilty of lying about it earlier this month. Yep, the debate is over—vaccines are safe! They always have been!

So what's causing the rise in autism rates? Oh, that was in the news recently, too. It turns out that older women who get pregnant have a higher risk for having a child with autism. This relates to a study from last year that showed older fathers are also at higher risk for producing an autistic child.

So you see, it's all the parents' fault. They were too busy with their careers or whatever and waited too late in life to have children, and this is the result. They got what they deserved.

So there's really no problem at all here. Vaccines are safe, reproduction is safe, and our children are safe. Everything's great. Look away. Now. There's nothing more to see here.

Have you stopped reading yet? Because most people usually do after only a paragraph or two, and that's why they come away believing the information stated above. It's a lot of misinformation and untruths, but I must have heard a dozen people parrot it back to me in the last month, regurgitating information they'd gotten from "reputable" news sources.

I can only partially blame the idiots who were so eager to share this information with me in the last month, as if it would somehow make me feel better about caring for my own autistic son. The rest of the blame has to lie with the lazy journalists who recycle information that is spoon-fed to them by governments and corporations without questioning it.

If you could get past the headline and opening graphs of the stories mentioned above you'd find the truth buried deep in the meat of these stories.

First, Dr. Andrew Wakefield, the English doctor who initially questioned the safety of the MMR (mumps/measles/rubella) shot in a 1998 Lancet article, was found guilty of unethical practices because he was paid by some of the parents of the children in his study to be an expert witness in their lawsuits against vaccine makers. He's guilty of a conflict of interest (though expert witnesses are often paid for their testimony in court—you don't think they do it for free, do you?).

But nobody found Dr. Wakefield's science invalid. The guy still found live mumps and measles viruses in the digestive tracts of the autistic children he studied. Other medical professionals verified his findings. If the viruses didn't come from the triple-whammy MMR shot, then where did they come from? How do you get rid of them? Why isn't anyone else asking these questions?

Speaking of the MMR shot, you may have heard another story recently about an ongoing mumps outbreak in New York and New Jersey that has sickened nearly 1,600 people. It turns out that 70 percent of the people who came down with the mumps had been vaccinated against it, giving rise to the question, *just how effective is the MMR shot, anyway?*

And the article on "older mothers at higher risk for autism" was another bit of non-news passed off as a revelation. Yes, women over 40 have a higher risk of having a child with autism. But it wasn't until the end of the article that it's revealed that women over 40 with autistic children make up less than five percent of the autistic population. So it's not like the autism rates have skyrocketed because women are waiting until they're older to reproduce. This article doesn't explain anything except what we already know – having a child later in life increases the risk for a variety of birth defects and developmental disorders, not just autism.

So what is causing the autism rates to rise to a point where 1-in-150 kids are being diagnosed? If it's not the vaccines then what is it?

Nobody knows. Despite funneling millions of dollars into research, scientists still don't have a clue. I think Dr. Andrew Wakefield gave them a good starting point twelve years ago—look to the brain/gut connection—but only a handful of scientists have followed his lead. The majority chose to make Wakefield their scapegoat instead, somebody to blame for causing a "false autism scare." The truth is that the autism epidemic is very real, and mainstream science, despite massive federal funding, has completely failed to come up with any satisfactory answers.

If you've made it this far…congratulations! Pat yourself on the back, most readers bailed out eight paragraphs ago. This article probably didn't get you any closer to understanding the cause of the autism epidemic, but then, neither did the other articles you read which promised autism news. At least you got a different perspective from the standard regurgitated autism info. I wish I had more for you. I wish the scientists, doctors, and journalists of the world had more for you, too.

And if you see me on the street, don't run up to me with "the big news" you recently heard about autism. I'll grab an MMR shot, and come after you with it.

But don't worry. It's completely safe and effective.

AUTISM DIVES INTO THE MAINSTREAM, BUT MISSES THE BOAT
Reprinted from Wayne TODAY, June 2010

It's been a tough year for parents of autistic children. I know because I am one, and the headlines and media reports about autism seem stacked against us.

The bad press started last year when the federal "vaccine court" ruled against parents of autistic children in a class action lawsuit. The parents were suing vaccine makers, claiming their mercury-containing shots caused their children's autism.

Then came reports of a "definitive" study refuting any link between autism and childhood vaccines, blaming all the controversy on one man, Dr. Andrew Wakefield, and his "shoddy science."

This was followed by reports that claimed one of the most popular "alternative treatments" for autism—

special diets—didn't work. Many parents of autistic children say removing gluten and dairy from their kids' diet results in better behavior and cognitive function, yet the "official" study found no benefit to an altered diet.

The take-home message of these stories is similar. Don't blame the rise in autism rates on vaccine makers or doctors, and don't waste time or money on special diets for autistic children. There's no validity to the brain-gut connection. It's a fallacy. The only thing that helps autistic kids is Applied Behavioral Analysis (ABA) therapy.

Personally, my wife and I found straight ABA Therapy, with its repetitive "discrete trials," disturbingly similar to the dog training we encountered when we volunteered at the animal shelter. We switched to a more language-based branch of ABA known as Verbal Behavior Therapy, instead.

As far as special diets go, like all autism treatments, some work great for certain children and have no effect on others. Our son was on a gluten-free/casein-free diet for nearly six years. Now we let him eat almost anything, but we give him digestive enzymes to help him break his food down. Despite what the official study says, digestive problems, feeding issues, and bizarre food-related behaviors are prevalent in the autistic community. For "researchers" to miss that means they looked too closely, not closely enough, or not at all.

The mainstream media has yielded some "clues" as to why autism rates are increasing around the world. First came reports that linked higher autism rates in children with older parents. Then came a study that pointed to a possible link between autism and infertility treatments. Autism rates were higher for parents who used in vitro fertilization and/or fertility pills to get pregnant.

Translation: Autism is the parents' fault. They waited until they were too old to have kids. They used unnatural methods to get pregnant, and now their kids are damaged. It's a shame these kids have to suffer, but really, the parents of autistic children have no one to blame but themselves.

Parents of special-needs kids used to at least get some sympathy for the extra challenges they faced. It was often quoted that 80 percent of parents of autistic children get divorced, a testament to the strain raising an autistic child puts on a marriage.

But a report released last month refutes this idea, too. A new study shows parents of autistic children *don't* get divorced more often than the parents of neuro-typical children. And if they *do* get divorced, it's often for some reason other than their special-needs child.

Translation: Parents of autistic children, who are always so tired, broke, and stressed out, are a bunch of whiners and complainers. They don't have it any harder than you or anyone else.

In addition to the articles and reports mentioned above, several articles have appeared in the mainstream media over the last year, many written by people with high-functioning autism and/or Asperger's syndrome, which encourage parents of autistic children to "leave your kids alone," and allow them to "be who they're going to be" without the interference of special education, therapies, diets, etc. They believe parents need to stop trying to "change" their autistic kids, and accept them for who they are.

Several primetime TV shows have included characters with Asperger's syndrome, including *Bones*, *Boston Legal*, and *Grey's Anatomy*. One of the characters on *Parenthood* is an eight-year-old boy with Asperger's syndrome. Some of these fictional portrayals are commendable in that they raise awareness of autism spectrum disorders, demystify the syndrome, and show the value of people who "think differently."

But all this "shiny, happy autism" stuff is annoying, because it's very different from the way my wife and I—and, I imagine many parents of autistic children—actually live. Sure, we have lots of happy moments with our son, but there are also a lot of really difficult ones, too. It's the hundred heartbreaking moments preceding the happy ones that make the good times seem so joyous when they arrive. It isn't until you've been knocked down flat that you can appreciate life's simple triumphs, like when your kid puts their shoes on the right feet, acts appropriately in a grocery store, or finally says, "I love you."

I think all this rah-rah autism reporting is a backlash against the Autism Speaks-sponsored film released a couple of years ago called *Autism Every Day*. The film followed the families of autistic children, and the challenges they face on a daily basis.

The problem was the film didn't show much else besides the challenges. It didn't show *any* love or joy. It didn't show laughter and family fun. It showed stressed-out, semi-suicidal parents and wild children. Lots of people, even the parents of autistic children, criticized the film for being too negative.

But now I believe the media is being "too positive" when it comes to autism. "There's nothing to fear...childhood vaccines are safe! There's no autism epidemic!" the reports seem to say, often failing to mention that autism rates have risen from 1-in-10,000 kids to 1-in-100 kids in the last two decades. "And if you *do* happen to get an autistic kid, it's no big deal. It won't put any extra strain on your marriage or family. Look at how happy the people on *Parenthood* are! In fact, your kid will probably grow up to be one of those quirky, lovable brainiacs, like on *The Big Bang Theory!*

Sure, some will do exactly that. But some will never get beyond collecting carts and bagging groceries at the local supermarket. Others will be unable to achieve even that. The spectrum of disorders that comprise autism is a wide one, with varying levels of skills and achievements. *Autism Every Day* seemed to focus on the wild end of the spectrum, while the current media trend is to focus in the mild side of the disorder.

But the truth--which varies from person to person, parent to parent, child to child--lies somewhere in the vast grey area between these two points.

Autism Dad

PART III—AUTISM & FAMILY

Your kid isn't the only one in the family transformed by autism. It affects each member of the family in his or her own way. Even the family pets.

One of Rocco's favorite pastimes is a game/stim we call "Rocco Errera: Doggy Dentist." Rocco likes to stare deeply into our dogs' mouths. He won't touch or hurt the dog; he just wants to look. His favorite patient was our old Shepherd mix, Barney. Rocco would stare into Barney's mouth for hours, studying his panting tongue and pointy teeth. He'd follow the dog around the house with a pillow. Sometimes poor Barney would hide in the basement just to escape Dr. Rocco's inquisitive glare.

Living with odd behaviors it what autism is all about. You put bad or destructive behaviors "on extinction," and adapt to the rest. Everybody in the family makes concessions for each other. In that way, being in an "autistic family" is no different than being in any other family. The circumstances are merely...weirder.

EXPLAINING AUTISM AND OTHER IMPOSSIBLE TASKS
Reprinted from Wayne TODAY, August 2007

I was lying in my daughter's bed, waiting for her to fall asleep. We'd finished reading (*Green Eggs and Ham* and *Goodnight Moon*), and I'd dimmed the light so she could drift off to sleep.

Francesca was babbling, scripting, talking softly in that endearing three-year-old voice of hers about what she did that day, what she planned to do tomorrow, and her general assessment of the world as she sees it ("Birds eat worms. Yuck. YUCK!"). She was quiet for several moments, and I figured she had fallen asleep, my cue to slip away and finish the nightly chores. But then she spoke again, and her words froze my heart.

"Rocco has...the autism," she said. Rocco is her five-year-old brother.

"Yes," I said.

"He's sick," she said.

"Yes, Francesca. He is."

"We have to help him…to make him better," she said.

Francesca spoke, but the words were her mother's. For the past week or so Francesca has been curious about the autism awareness symbols she sees around our house—the puzzle-piece t-shirt and necklace her mother wears, the bumper sticker on our car. Her mother must have explained it to her.

I knew this day was coming, but it still arrived too soon. How do you explain to a child that their sibling has autism? Autism, which often has few physical characteristics and lots of inexplicable "weird" behaviors, is hard enough for adults to understand. How will a child ever get it?

But even at age three my daughter knows there is something different about her older brother. He doesn't play the way other children do. After a recent visit with her typical cousin, Francesca remarked, "Rocco doesn't play with me like Jackie does."

There's a long road ahead for Francesca, as there is for all siblings of autistic children. In a "normal" sibling relationship there are ongoing shifts in feelings of resentment, jealousy, embarrassment, pride, affection and companionship. When your sibling has autism—or any of a number of other disabilities, for that matter—those feelings are all magnified.

Over the course of her lifetime, Francesca will undoubtedly face a number of other feelings concerning her "special sibling," feelings like guilt, anger, shame, sorrow, and confusion. The sibling relationship is the longest relationship in a family, so sibling issues are lifelong issues that change throughout the lifespan.

Lying there in the dark, hearing my daughter say the word "autism" in a tiny voice as delicate as blown glass, I'm filled with my own blend of anger and sorrow. Why does she have to know about this, now, at such a young age? And how will having an autistic sibling impact her when she's five, ten, fifteen or twenty? How about when she's forty or fifty? What does the future hold for any of us?

Suddenly I'm glad I dimmed the light in my daughter's room. The look on my face, the tears in my eyes, might frighten her.

"Yes, Francesca, your brother has autism," I whisper to her in the dark. "But we'll help him. We'll help make him better."

"Yeah," she replies dreamily, her thoughts already drifting to the next topic and the one beyond. In a few moments her breathing slows, and she is asleep.

I lie awake in the dark for a long time.

JENNY MCCARTHY JOINS ARMY OF WARRIOR MOMS
Reprinted from Wayne TODAY, October 2007

Something happens to a woman when her child is diagnosed with autism.

Her heart breaks, of course. Some stay broken forever.

But sometimes the heart of an "autism mom" heals in strange ways. It's tougher than it was before, and has a greater capacity for love. There are other changes, too. Their brains grow as they soak up knowledge about the disorder that has gripped their children. Whatever their job was before autism, they all become experts on behavioral therapy and biochemistry. Their voices get loud as they advocate for their kids. Their spines turn to steel.

These are the "warrior moms" on the front lines of the fight against autism. Autism has stolen their children, but their fierce love and determination is going to bring them back. Failure is not an option. They won't take no for an answer.

My wife is a warrior mom. She knew our son was autistic even before a doctor officially diagnosed him. Our pediatrician gave our son a clean bill of health at his 18-month check-up, even though my wife told him our son didn't always respond to his name, and didn't play appropriately with toys.

My wife Googled into the night until she found the CHAT test for autism (Checklist For Autism in Toddlers), a five-minute questionnaire designed to highlight possible autistic markers in young children. My son failed many of the checkpoints. My wife Googled "curing autism," and found information about a gluten-free/casein-free diet.

My son was already wheat free for a week before a developmental pediatrician formally diagnosed him with autism. My wife asked the doctor what he thought of the GF/CF diet. He told her it was a waste of time. She smiled politely and thanked the doctor for his opinion. She took our son off dairy the next day. Two weeks later his eye contact was better, and he started pointing again.

This was the start of my wife's autism odyssey. She has not made the journey alone. In the four years we've been treating our son's autism, my wife has aligned herself with an army of autism moms across the nation. They network via phone, email and message boards, swapping information about treatments, doctors, therapists, and research. If you want to research the latest, most cutting-edge treatments for autism, this network of warrior moms will know more than most doctors, even ones that specialize in autism.

Jenny McCarthy is a warrior mom, too. Her book, *Louder than Words: A Mother's Journey in Healing Autism* is an excellent account of how McCarthy lost her son to autism, and the lengths she goes to in order to bring him back. Before McCarthy can help her son, she herself is rescued by the autism moms she meets at her son's new school. These women look past McCarthy's *Playboy*-centerfold looks and celebrity status and treat her as one of their own, acknowledging her grief, sharing their knowledge about treatments, and filling her with hope not offered by the traditional medical community.

McCarthy's story is a familiar one to parents of autistic children. My wife and I could relate to nearly all of it. Anguish over our son's autism diagnosis? Yes. Arguing with pediatricians over the cause and/or treatment of autism? Been there, done that. Financial problems? Marital problems? Check. Check. Making autism the all-consuming center of your life while once-important things—like family, friends, and careers—fade away? You betcha. Finding hope in alternative treatments for autism? Yes.

In fact, Jenny McCarthy's story could have been our own with one major difference. Her son recovered from autism; ours hasn't yet. Our son has improved, but hasn't made the big leaps like McCarthy's kid. Biomedical treatments for autism don't work for every kid.

But you've got to try and keep trying. That's what warriors do.

I have a newfound respect for Jenny McCarthy. It takes guts to come out publicly in favor of biomedical treatments for autism, knowing that 95 percent of the traditional medical community will say you're wrong, crazy, or both. It's braver still to stand against the Centers for Disease Control, and denounce their schedule for childhood vaccines. But Jenny knows the truth needs to be told; something is stealing our kids (at a rate of 1-in-150 and climbing) but there are treatments that can help bring them back. Preach it, Jenny. You go, girl!

My respect for Jenny McCarthy is topped only by my respect for my wife. I don't tell her that often enough, but I should. She is my hero. She's worked longer and harder than Ms. McCarthy, but has only seen a fraction of the results. She's got the heart of a warrior; she keeps fighting for our son. She's also way hotter than Jenny McCarthy.

Awesome proofreader, too.

ENDNOTE: My wife is awesome. She's like a superhero, moving mountains through sheer force of will. She's certainly my hero. I wouldn't be Autism Dad without her. I wouldn't be anything.

When I wrote this column in the fall of 2007, I had no idea Jenny McCarthy would call her next book, Warrior Moms. *Great minds think alike!*

One of the most valuable things my wife does is share her knowledge with others. Through her circle of "autism moms," she's met dozens of women whose children were recently diagnosed with autism spectrum disorder. She'd cry with these women, grieve with them, and then offer advice on how to "deal with it," suggesting dietary changes and behavioral therapy that could help their kids. She truly is a "warrior mom," fighting not only for our own kid, but for all *the kids we know who are affected by ASD.*

But what about Autism Dads?

We're a hard-working bunch, but we don't roll the way the ladies do. We don't gather in clusters, commiserate, and swap gluten-free recipes. Too bad, in a way – it might help.

But guys are wired differently. We're rogues. We keep our pain inside. The few times I've gotten together with groups of Autism Dads, they've been awkward affairs, a bunch of dudes standing around embarrassed until somebody breaks the ice by talking about sports or power tools. Maybe these affairs are so strange because Autism Dads are a little bit autistic and socially weird themselves. That's the excuse I use. Warrior Moms bind together to fight a Great War. Autism Dads fight a more private battle.

MOMMY'S FEET, STICKER BOOK, AND OTHER TERMS OF ENDEARMENT
Reprinted from Wayne TODAY, July 2009

When your kid has autism, communication breakdowns are an everyday occurrence.

Communication problems are a common thread across the wide spectrum of autism disorders. Some people with autism are completely non-verbal. Others have limited vocabulary. Even those with a grasp of speech and language often have trouble reading social cues and carrying on a conversation.

Words and sounds are sometimes used to communicate in rather non-traditional ways. My son, Rocco, does a variation of the Tarzan yell that can be quite an attention grabber, especially in supermarkets and shopping malls. He'll change his pitch depending on his mood, so it *is* an expressive sound. But sometimes I think he's making sounds to block out background noise, and help him focus on what he's doing.

Sometimes my son talks in code. He'll say one thing, but mean another. Or he'll say something that seemingly makes no sense.

When he's happy, he'll blurt out the phrase, "Mommy's feet!" When he's unhappy, he'll say "car book," or "truck book," or "sticker book." He'll use all three phrases in some situations, and only certain ones in others, but I haven't quite unraveled the nuances of the appropriate use of each phrase. He wanted to go outside the other day and I told him he had to wait. He looked at me and said, "sticker book." I'm sure he intended it to mean something quite vulgar.

I found myself explaining these things recently to various family members during our annual trip to the Jersey shore. Sharing a beach house with 10-20 people can be a bit overwhelming for anybody, but especially so for a kid with autism. Plus, Roc's Tarzan yell is a way of life for my wife and daughter and I; it's the soundtrack of our lives, and we barely notice it. But I imagine it's probably irritating to others, especially those used to quieter living arrangements.

That's another thing about raising a child with autism, or any special-needs child for that matter. Occasions that are supposed to be "fun"—like holidays and birthdays and summer vacations—are often a drag. They break the routine, set behavioral expectations that are often hard to meet, and they tend to underscore the developmental milestones your child's *missed,* rather than the ones they have achieved. Birthdays can be especially difficult.

Summer vacations are no picnic either. We've had some disastrous ones. When he was three, Rocco escaped from the rental house, and snuck down to the beach for a solo swim. We found him hanging out on the beach with a bunch of kindly strangers (angels) who had fished him out of the surf. The following year he had a meltdown in a public park. Another year, both my kids did so much damage to the rental house, Grandma had to find a different house to rent the next year. As much as I love seeing my Mom, my siblings and their families, there were some years when I couldn't wait for our summer vacation to end.

This year wasn't one of them. My wife and kids and I all had a great time – we even stayed an extra day. The beach was a blast; the skies were blue, the sun was ripe, and the waves were just right.

Rocco and I played in the surf. He greeted each crashing breaker with a squeal of delight. Imagine a pre-pubescent Tarzan just getting the hang of riding the vines. We were probably drawing stares from our fellow beachgoers, but I didn't care. We were having fun.

"Daddy!" My son gripped my hand.

"What is it, buddy?"

"Happy," he said.

"What?" I said. "Say it again, Roc."

Not because I didn't understand him, but because I did, and it sounded so beautiful.

"Daddy," he said. "I'm happy!"

"I'm happy too, son," I told him. "I'm happy too."

I didn't need a secret decoder ring to figure this one out. Sometimes the words are just right.

Mommy's feet.

BEDTIME JAM BAND A REWARDING GIG
Reprinted from Wayne TODAY, July 2010

I'm pleased to report that after an extended musical hiatus, I am once again a member of a band. We don't play out anywhere, but we rehearse nightly in my son's bedroom.

It's a duo, just Rocco and me. The name of the band is Buddy Club.

Buddy Club began as more of a gender-exclusive social club within our home, a counterpart to the Secret Society of Girlfriends, which my wife and daughter belong to. It didn't become a musical act until later, as a way to both interact with my son, and to help him settle down for bed. It's become a rewarding gig for both of us.

My son is eight, and has autism. Finding things for us to do together is sometimes a challenge. Aside from some jigsaw puzzles, my son doesn't like playing games. He's a sensory-driven kid. He likes bouncing on the trampoline and hanging upside-down, activities my middle-aged body can only take so much of. Music—both listening and playing—is one of a handful of activities my son and I enjoy together.

My son often has a hard time, "putting himself down" for the night, so last year I tried playing guitar for him before bed. It didn't make Rocco go to sleep any quicker, but he did seem to enjoy the music. He'd often flip through books while I played. (Another Rocco quirk: he likes books but he doesn't like being read to or reading aloud. You're welcome to *watch* him read a book, just don't interrupt or attempt to interact with him – he'll pitch a fit.)

Some nights I'd lose myself in a tune, closing my eyes while I sang and played. When I opened my eyes at the end of the song, I'd often find Rocco staring at me. He was listening and paying attention in a way he rarely did.

I brought in instruments for Rocco to play. I added another guitar, a harmonica, a tambourine, and a shaker. Sometimes Rocco would play them, sometimes not. Sometimes he'd lie in bed and beat a rhythm on the wall with his feet, other times he'd sit and look at books while I played.

He contributes vocals, too, though it's often either a whispered script ("Once upon a time, there were three little pigs..." goes with chord progressions both happy and sad) or a loud nonsensical "Tarzan yell."

One night during rehearsal, Rocco was vocalizing so loudly, I stopped playing and put my finger to my lips to quiet him down. Rocco looked shocked and a little hurt, and he was right. All day long people stifle his inappropriate vocal stims; band rehearsal is the one place where he should be able to make whatever kind of noise, at whatever level of volume, he wants. I never hushed him again after that night. Now, if he blurts something out during a song, I encourage it.

"Sounds good, Buddy...let's hear some more."

Our sets are eclectic, mostly classic rock with a few blues standards and original tunes worked in. We open every rehearsal with an A-minor chord; for some reason my son likes the way my fingers look when I chicken-pick this chord. Sometimes we'll go on a random jam from there, other times I'll lead into a trio of thematically and/or musically similar tunes. Prince's "Purple Rain," Peter Gabriel's "Red Rain," and the Eurythmics' "Here Comes The Rain Again, " for example.

Sometimes Roc sings and plays along, other times he watches and listens, sometimes he reads books, and sometimes he'll stick his foot in the sound hole of my guitar. He doesn't always do this to make me stop playing. Sometimes he wants to feel the vibrations of the guitar strings against his skin as I strum. Like I said, he's a sensory kid.

Sometimes he'll stop me mid-tune and place his head against mine.

"I want you to purr," he'll say, and I'll do it, rolling my tongue until both our heads are filled with the motor-like vibrations. Other times he'll want me to scratch his feet or tickle his armpit. Rarely do we ever go back to the interrupted song. After a sensory break, we'll try a different musical number, a freeform jam, or even a drum solo, slapped out bare-handed on the body of the guitar, sometimes with a shaker or tambourine accompaniment. Some nights there's lots of music with few sensory breaks. Other nights, rehearsal is more like one long sensory session with occasional music tossed in. You have to go with the flow, play loosey-goosey with the rules, and improvise often.

In that way, making music with an autistic kid is a lot like *raising* an autistic kid. You have to plan and schedule more than with a neuro-typical kid, yet you have to be willing to toss all that prep work out the window, and go with Plan B, C, or Z at a moment's notice. You have to encourage appropriate behavior, and put inappropriate behavior "on extinction."

You have to be alert for "teaching moments" when they come up. My son is super-smart and learns quickly if he's genuinely interested, but it's tough to generate a passion for learning unless he feels it. You can teach him things, but it has to be on his terms. When he's ready, you'd better be, too.

You have to grab "bonding moments" when they come, and hold onto them like they're the most important things in the world.

Because they are.

"My buddy," Rocco will sometimes interrupt a Buddy Club rehearsal to tell me.

"Of course," I reply. "Always."

"My buddy," he'll say again, wanting me to repeat it back.

"You're my buddy," I tell him.

"Pawprints," he says.

I don't know what "pawprints" have to do with anything, but Rocco always adds it at the close of our "my buddy" exchange. I like to think it's his version of, "I love you," but who knows. Maybe he's calling me an idiot.

Rocco isn't the strangest musician I've ever jammed with, nor is he the least accomplished. His harmonica playing is quite soulful when the mood strikes him. I've played with musicians in college who were even more moody, quirky, and unpredictable than my son, but not nearly as much fun to be around. And I've been in plenty of bands that never made it out of the garage, basement, bedroom—wherever our rehearsal space might be.

But, unlike before, I don't really care if Buddy Club ever lands a gig beyond my son's bedroom. This isn't about making money, getting famous, or even entertaining anyone beyond ourselves. It's about forging a bond, a bond with someone who sometimes has difficulty forming them. It's about making a joyful noise.

It's about pawprints.

WHAT'S FOR DINNER? BAKED CELL PHONE AND STEAMED DAD
Reprinted from Wayne TODAY, September 2010

My son's name is Rocco, but Conan the Destroyer would be more apt. The boy has an appetite for destruction.

And he's always hungry.

Rocco's autism is a factor in his destructive behavior. He often uses items in inappropriate ways, like raiding my wallet and using the credit cards in an origami display (the plastic card in the cable box folds nicely, too!), or mixing a concoction of cinnamon and onion powder over the toaster (which makes for funky waffles). Autism accounts for some of these behaviors, but I think even if Rocco were a typical kid he'd have a destructive streak. He likes to see how things are put together...and how they come apart.

Electronics are his favorite. He toasted a not-so-Toughbook, and destroyed several iPods. Wireless phones are a constant terror target. I knew trouble was brewing the afternoon I called my wife's cell phone and Rocco answered. He was laughing wildly, and I heard water running in the background.

"Buddy?" I said. "Hey, Roc! Give Mommy the phone."

He laughed and hung up. I called back, but got no answer. I sent a text.

'Roc's got your phone. Not a toy!'

No reply...until I got home that night.

"Bad news," my wife said, shortly after I walked through the front door. "Want it now?"

I didn't, but my six-year-old daughter spilled the beans.

"Rocco took Mommy's phone into the shower," she said. "Now it doesn't work."

This *was* bad news. Mom's phone was a re-activated older model, because her new phone broke under "unknown circumstances." The old flip phone had a cracked front screen, surrounded by mysterious teeth marks, but otherwise worked fine.

Until today.

Now the phone was a soggy mess, the tiny space behind the screen filled with water, a lifeless aquarium.

"Did you put it in rice?" I asked. This wasn't our first wireless phone to take a swim. We'd rescued submersed phones before by tossing them in a bag of rice, which absorbs the moisture.

"We don't have any rice."

What now? A hair dryer? That would be loud, tedious work. I am a self-proclaimed "Daddy Who Fixes Things," and I try hard to live up to the title. But this was a tough fix.

"Maybe we could put it in the oven, bake it at, say, 100 degrees?" I suggested.

It was worth a try. We removed the battery and baked the phone for a few hours. We tried it later, and the screen powered up, misted with internal condensation. The buttons still weren't working, so we turned the oven off and left the phone in there overnight.

My wife tried it again the next morning. The phone powered up, and she ran through the menus, gave it a test run.

"Wow. Everything works," she smiled. "You're my hero."

I felt like one, too. It's not every man who can resurrect a drowned cell phone from a watery grave. Only a Daddy Who Fixes Things.

"There's a new text message," my wife said, clicking it open. "Yes, Rocco's got my phone...no, it's not a toy..."

PART IV—AUTISM'S OBSTACLES

Being a parent means making tough decisions. Being the parent of a special-needs child means making tough decisions *all the time*. You have to constantly stay on top of what your child needs, both socially and educationally. And, let's be honest, sometimes your kid's communication deficiencies make it hard to know exactly *what* he wants or needs. You try to make the best decisions you can, but sometimes you're guessing blind.

Parents of autistic children must clear many hurdles during the course of raising their child, everything from fighting with school boards and government agencies, to enduring the withering stares of their neighbors if your kid has a meltdown. The deepest battle scars often occur when you find yourself facing off against an opponent you thought was an ally.

THE "ASHLEY TREATMENT" DRAWS PRAISE; SCORN
Reprinted from Wayne TODAY, January 2007

Ashley is a nine-year-old girl who will never grow up. Her parents have made sure of it by having her uterus and breast tissue removed, and flooding her with hormones to ensure she remains in a child-like body.

Why would her parents do such a thing? Ashley has severe brain damage and developmental disabilities. Her condition has left her in an infant-like state, unable to sit up, roll over, walk, or talk. Her parents, who believe Ashley's condition will never improve, decided to undergo this radical "growth stunting" procedure so that Ashley would forever remain "small and portable." Ashley will never grow larger than 4'5" and top out at a weight of 75 pounds – about a foot shorter and 50 pounds lighter than a typical adult female.

"Ashley's smaller and lighter size makes it more possible to include her in the typical family," her parents wrote on their Internet blog. Her parents also say that keeping Ashley small will reduce the risk of bedsores and other conditions that can afflict bedridden patients. She'll also never go through puberty, so she won't experience the discomfort of periods or grow breasts that might develop breast cancer, which runs in her family.

Since news of "The Ashley Treatment" broke earlier this month, medical "ethicists" and news pundits around the globe have debated the issue. Some feel Ashley's parents are horrible monsters that are playing God for their own convenience. Others support their decision, claiming it is both a sensible and humane way to ensure their daughter lives the most comfortable life possible. As Ashley's parents point out, the only people who have the right to comment on their decision are other parents of disabled children. "Unless you are living the experience, you are speculating, and you have no clue what it is like to be the bedridden child or their caregivers," they write.

Well, I'm the parent of a child with permanent disabilities; my son has autism. While this is far from the "bedridden hell" Ashley and her parents must endure, having an autistic child is still quite a challenge. My wife and I hope that Rocco's autism won't be permanent—we're trying everything possible to recover our son. One of the mysteries of autism, especially when your child is young, is that you don't know how it's going to turn out, just how disabling this disability will be. Autism is a spectrum disorder, meaning some people are deeply affected by it, others only mildly. Rocco's future is uncertain, as are the futures of many children with autism.

Rocco is also an exceptionally cute kid. Like, baby-supermodel cute. I sound like a boastful Dad, but it's true. Rocco's a handsome little boy. Frankly, I think Rocco's good looks have helped him overcome some of the barriers of autism. His blue eyes and brilliant smile get him extra attention from the "ladies" in his life: his Mom, his teachers, and his female classmates. Chicks dig Rocco. If he needs extra help with something, he always gets it.

But this might not always be the case. I've met autistic children of all ages. The trend seems to be that the young ones are really cute. But by the time they hit adolescence, they start to look…different. They look like there's something wrong with them. The gap of social acceptance becomes wider, grows along with the rest of the delays, and gets harder to bridge. The breaks that come to all the beautiful people in this world stop coming.

So, if I knew Rocco was never going to get better, that he would always have the mind of a child, would

I keep him in the body of a child, too, if given the choice?

I don't know. That's a hard question to even consider. Part of me thinks I'd do it; I might keep my child a "forever child" if he were never going to get better.

But another part of me questions "The Ashley Treatment." What will the mental and physical effects be as Ashley ages but doesn't grow? What will the psychological and physical effects be on her family? Ashley's parents are betting that the long-term benefits to their daughter's overall health and quality of life will outweigh these potential pitfalls. They're making choices now that permanently affect their daughter's life forever. They're making hard choices.

To a certain degree, this is the job of every parent, whether your child is typical, special-needs, or severely disabled. You have to constantly make choices—about what your kid eats, where they go to school, what they watch on TV, etc. Sometimes these choices reverberate, affecting your child's life for years to come. Sometimes you don't know you've made a bad choice until it's too late. You try to make the best decisions you can; fill your head with knowledge, and keep your heart wide open. That's what Ashley's parents did. You don't have to be an ethicist to see these people are doing what they believe is best for their child.

That's all anyone can ask of a parent.

SPECIAL ED CRISIS: THE HIGH COST OF AUTISM EDUCATION
Reprinted from Wayne TODAY, April 2008

Here's a story within a story within a story.

The first story starts with a local headline: "Escalating Special Ed Costs Impact Surplus." The Bloomingdale, NJ Board of Ed recently had to move $238,000 from its $343,447 surplus to cover special education services. They also appropriated an additional $50,000 to pay litigation costs related to special education services.

Although matters of pending litigation could not be discussed, the story behind the story was clear: Bloomingdale is spending a boatload of money on Special Ed services, but it's not enough. Evidently some parents want additional services, and are willing to take the borough to court.

Bloomingdale Board of Ed member Dan Schlotterbeck feels the state should help shoulder the cost of some of these services.

"These are necessary costs," he said. "But we can't do it alone."

And that's where the story within the story lays—the big story. Special education costs are on the rise across the nation. Why? Autism rates are on the rise. An estimated 1-in-150 kids are being diagnosed with the developmental disorder. Nowhere is this felt more acutely than in New Jersey, where the rate of this disorder is 1-in-94; 1-in-60 boys in the state of New Jersey are being diagnosed with autism. That's a lot of special education students. That's a lot of special education students who have *yet to be born*.

Nearly eight years ago, the Government Accountability Office estimated the cost of educating an autistic child at $18,000 per year, nearly three times the cost of educating a typical student. It costs more to educate an autistic student than any other type of special education student. And states are mandated to educate autistic students until the age of 21.

It all adds up to a financial crisis that could bankrupt any educational system. It's a financial crisis that's already upon us, only its effects have yet to be fully felt. The Bloomingdale school board feels the pinch. They won't be first. Things are going to get much worse.

My son has autism, so I have firsthand knowledge of educating an autistic child. So far it has been a financial hot potato—a responsibility that everyone wants to quickly toss off to someone else. The state school board wants local towns to educate autistic students in-district; let each individual school board figure out how to pay for its autistic kids. But the smaller districts, like Bloomingdale (and the one I live in) aren't equipped to handle the educational needs of ASD (Autism Spectrum Disorder) and PDD-NOS (Pervasive Developmental Disorder-Not Otherwise Specified) classified kids, so they look for out-of-district placements; they pay somebody else to educate their autistic kids.

But even if the price tag is high, the services can be sub-standard. The demand for a quality education for autistic children is simply overwhelming the supply; too many kids need help and there are not enough qualified staff to help them. I can sympathize with the parents of special-needs kids in Bloomingdale, the ones who are alluded to only between the lines of the story about school board bookkeeping. It costs a lot to educate an autistic student, but autism is such an individualized disorder that sometimes your kid still needs more.

Sometimes you have to fight to get it.

BONUS ESSAY—AUTISM ETIQUETTE FOR DUMMIES

I'm looking for a book about autism etiquette, but I can't seem to find one. I felt there was a need for such a book, so I figured I'd write it myself.

Then I realized, I really don't know squat. As the father of an autistic child, I find myself facing autism etiquette questions every day, sometimes several times a day.

And I usually get them wrong.

Who am I to write a book about autism etiquette? The best I can do is this essay—even that's iffy.

What is autism etiquette? It's the way people act and react when they're around people with autism. It's also about the way parents react to their child's autism, and how they present themselves and their child to the world.

For the most part, you can't control the behavior of your autistic child—or any kid for that matter. (Though we are forever trying to change the behavior of autistic children through modification therapy, like applied behavioral analysis [ABA].)

A parent can only control the way they *react* to their child's behavior. And a parent's reaction is often the best guide for how others will act toward your kid. Lead by example.

That being said, sometimes my leadership is weak. When I'm out with my son I try to go with the flow, blend in, and not draw attention to his eccentric behavior. Maybe I should be more upfront with people.

But when—and how—do you tell people your child has autism? I'm not talking about family and friends. I'm talking about strangers, people you meet as part of your daily routine.

This is a more complex question than it seems, and, of course, the answer depends on the scenario. Autism is a strange disability on many levels, but primarily because it doesn't *look* like anything. To the untrained eye, an autistic kid looks likes a regular child being a brat, throwing a tantrum, or acting weird.

How do you handle someone who's watching your kid act up in public?

Here are some good suggestions I've found on the Internet:

"My son has autism. What's the reason for your behavior?"

"Oh, I'm sorry, I hope he is not disturbing you. You see, he has autism, and he is still learning to ...talk, wait in line, act appropriately, etc."

"My son has autism, and he is trying his best. Please understand, he can't communicate like you and I, and it's very frustrating. It's like visiting a foreign country, not understanding the customs or language, yet being expected to function."

"I tell my son, 'Stop, you're scaring the straights.*' This has a two-fold effect: my son usually stops his odd behavior, and the people around us are made aware of their reaction."*

"When my son acts up in public, I just say as loudly as I can, 'Please excuse me everybody, my son is having an autism moment.'"

"My son is autistic. Please keep him in your prayers."

Those are all pretty good, and work in a variety of situations. Here's one I came up with:

"My son has autism, so he might not say much, or react the way you expect, but I'm pretty sure he understands everything you say."

Rocco's receptive language is pretty good, and I believe he *does* understand most of what I'm saying. Either way, I want people to *treat him* like he understands.

Still, there are awkward moments. Once at the park, Rocco took the hand of an older girl, and led her to the see-saw.

"My son has autism, and he loves the see-saw," I said. "It's the up-and-down motion. He'll keep you there all day if you let him, so feel free to stop at any time."

The girl looked a little bewildered, but kept smiling. Did I say the wrong thing? Should I not have said anything at all, and let her figure it out? They see-sawed for a few minutes. Roc broke it off first, and that was that. In hindsight, I probably didn't have to say anything at all. He could have just been a quiet kid playing with another kid.

My wife handles things differently than I. She addresses our son's autism right away, and politely relates it to the situation at hand.

"My son has autism, so can you seat us at a table where we won't bother anyone?"

"My son has autism, and doesn't like loud noises."

"Sorry my son is rifling through your shopping cart. He has autism."

My wife's approach is to the point, and gets the issue of my son's autism out of the way. But I'm not convinced it's entirely correct. I've read several anecdotes from autistic adults who felt their moms did them a disservice by always associating their autism with negative things ("he's autistic, so he can't speak, he doesn't like bright lights," etc.). They would have preferred their mothers occasionally refer to their "autistic brain power." I'll have to try that one sometime.

I feel my son's autism is on a "need to know" basis. If I feel it will help resolve a complicated social situation, I'll tell people he has autism. But sometimes you don't feel like explaining everything to a layperson. And you *definitely* don't feel like explaining it to some pinhead you pass in the supermarket, giving you the hairy eyeball because your kid is screeching like a banshee, or grabbing cans off the shelves.

Some parents solve this problem by putting their kids in "autism awareness" T-shirts. There are plenty of cute ones: "I'm not a brat, I'm autistic," and "Think you're having a bad day? Try having autism!" among them.

But the flipside to the autism T-shirt solution is that it can make autistic kids look like they're wearing a scarlet letter. After all, you don't see people walking around with T-shirts that read, "I Have Dementia," or

"Hug Me, I'm Bi-Polar." Why should kids with autism have to, literally, wear their disorder on their sleeve?

My wife understands the arguments made by the anti-autism T-shirt crowd, but as she puts it, "It's a good option if you're going somewhere, and don't feel like explaining your kid's behaviors to everyone."

What was the most important thing I learned while researching my autism etiquette book?

That there's no need for one...at least there shouldn't be. Treat an autistic person with the same attention, respect, and dignity you'd show a neurologically-typical person. You might not get the response you expect. You might not get any response at all. But do it anyway. And keep trying. Be patient and persistent, and you and your new autistic friend will both feel better. Autistic children (and adults) want the acceptance of their peers, just like anyone else.

Lots of autistic people have trouble making eye contact, but that doesn't mean you should. Look kids with autism in the eye, and greet them with a warm, welcoming smile.

Even though a child with autism may seem like he's ignoring you, he's probably not. Either way, don't do the same to him.

Talk to autistic kids at an age-appropriate level. Don't talk down to them. Just because a child with autism may have the vocabulary of a two-year-old, doesn't mean he has the mind of one.

Kids with autism can be very sensitive to moods and behaviors. If you're tense and nervous they'll pick up on that, and they'll be tense and nervous too. Relax and take the pressure off. Everyone will feel more at ease.

You're the adult, and kids – both autistic and typical – look to you for social cues. So do their parents. Set a good example. The world will be a better place for it.

BONUS ESSAY—THE LEGEND OF LEAD HOUSE

The state government kicked my family out of our house. We drifted like nomads, homeless.

No, we didn't fail to pay our taxes or mortgage. They kicked us out of our home because they wanted to *help* us. Really.

We've tried a lot of alternative therapies while treating our son's autism. For a while we were doing chelation therapy, which is supposed to remove heavy metals from my son's system. To ensure

Rocco's liver and kidneys could handle the treatment, we had his blood tested every six months.

One of those tests revealed elevated levels of lead in Rocco's blood. The levels were so high, the state health department was notified. The local health officer came out, and took dust samples from around our house. Yes, there was old lead paint around our windows and in our front porch. We would need "lead remediation" in several areas of the house.

"All based on the results of one blood draw?" I asked. "What if the lab made a mistake?"

We tested Roc's blood dozens of times, both before and after the state got involved. The elevated lead levels were never repeated. One of Rocco's doctors suggested the chelation therapy was working, and he was experiencing a massive lead dump.

"No, your kid ate a paint chip," my Lead Remediation Project Manager said. "The paint samples came back positive for lead."

"According to the literature you gave me, most houses built prior to 1970 have lead paint."

"But they don't have kids testing positive for lead toxicity living in them. And now that this is officially on record you have no choice but to get lead remediation. You'll need to replace every window in the house, and get your front porch rebuilt."

"What? I don't have the money for that!"

"Well, the Department of Community Affairs has some very good low interest loans available for lead remediation..."

So began one of the most harrowing and intrusive ordeals my family has ever endured (and, as parents of an autistic child, we're not unfamiliar with hardship and heartache). Our case was handed over to a lead abatement specialist at Lew Corp. (a contractor that watches *other* contractors remove lead, and reports back to the state). Lew Corp. did its own lead assessment of our home, and outlined a detailed remediation plan. They gave us a list of state-approved lead remediation contractors. We had to get three bids and pick one.

Every contractor who bid on the job informed us we had asbestos shingles on our house. If the shingles cracked and crumbled, they could be just as toxic as lead. The state didn't see it that way. They'd only give us a loan for the lead work; we'd have to pay for asbestos removal and new siding ourselves. We borrowed even more money from family members.

The terms of the DCA loan were pretty good. It was a forgivable loan payable over 20 years. If we lived in the house the next two decades, the loan was considered paid in full. If we sold after ten years, we'd have to pay back half, if we sold after five years, we'd owe three-quarters of the loan, etc. The money in the state's lead abatement fund came from taxes added to every can of paint.

The loan seemed like a pretty good deal. Our front porch was in dire need of repair, and I couldn't afford to fix it any other way. Besides, I wasn't given much choice.

"What happens if I refuse to have this work done?" I asked.

"Well, sir, your son is already on file with the state as being lead poisoned. This would be considered an unsafe home for your child, and then the Division of Youth and Family Services would get involved..."

Fine. We signed the DCA's 20-year loan, and picked a contractor over the summer. Work was scheduled to begin in late August.

We had to relocate during the construction, and put all of our stuff in a storage unit. Fortunately, we were able to move into my in-laws' house. They were snowbirds, and wouldn't be back from Florida until the holidays. That gave us plenty of time. The job was only supposed to take four weeks.

It took four months.

The beginning was the worst. I wasn't there the morning the workmen arrived. But I got a call from a friend around mid-day.

"Hey, bro! I drove by your house today, and there were six guys in spacesuits crawling all over it. It looked like a haz-mat scene!"

I drove by that night. The workmen were gone, but the place looked like the scene at the end of *E.T.: The Extra-Terrestrial* when scientists descend upon the suburban home, and turn it into a sterilized military zone. The entire house was wrapped in plastic. There were "Danger: Lead Contamination" signs on our front yard. A portable decontamination shower was set up in the backyard.

I went inside. Thick plastic sheeting covered all the walls and floors. Doorways were sealed with plastic and tape. It didn't even look like our house. It looked like a place where something terrible and poisonous had happened, a crime scene. I felt like crying.

We live on a main road, so by the next day the entire town had seen the haz-mat crew crawling all over our house. My wife and I were mortified. What would our neighbors think? What would this do to local property values? We'd *have* to live in the house for the next twenty years to live down this level of public shame. None of this was mentioned in the terms of the DCA's loan.

Moving to the in-laws' house wasn't smooth sailing either. One morning Roc woke early, unlocked the front door, and took a stroll around the new neighborhood. Since we were new, nobody knew whom he belonged to, or where he lived. Rocco stuck to the sidewalk, but he crossed a busy side street several times, according to the nice neighbor lady who followed him around for half an hour. He wouldn't tell her his name, or where he lived, but she stayed with him anyway. Eventually, Rocco walked back home. I found him and the neighbor lady sitting in our kitchen when I woke up.

"Is he yours?" she asked.

"Uh...yeah," I said. My eyes were still filled with sleep, my arms full of our obese dog. I carried her downstairs each morning because she was too big to make it on her own.

"He was walking up and down the street."

"Oh, my God! I'm sorry! We just moved in...this is my in-laws' house...we're having work done...he has autism..."

I was babbling. The woman smiled.

"I figured as much. I live next door," she said. She introduced herself. "Your son's very cute," she said before she left.

He's adorable, I thought, but he's killing me. Thank you again, lady. This was every parent's worst nightmare. You brought it to a safe end.

The men in spacesuits were gone a few weeks later. Now our home looked like any other house under renovation. But the project hit snags, delays with plans and permits. The gas company had to re-route a line. Fall was turning to winter and the work still wasn't done. My in-laws would be home for Christmas in a few weeks and we needed to get out of their house and back to ours.

The project wrapped up right after Thanksgiving, but before we moved back, we wanted to repaint the interior walls and refinish the floors. The outside of the house looked good – new siding and windows – and we wanted the inside to match. But since we were broke, we did the work ourselves. That took another three weeks, working like dogs every night and weekend. We moved back home the day before my in-laws arrived, one week before Christmas. It was a crazy holiday, moving boxes and Christmas presents battling for space in our living room.

Is all well that ends well? I suppose. The renovations to our home *are* pretty nice, the place looks spiffy, and we wouldn't have done it otherwise. (Let's be honest, if we had $70,000 lying around, it would have gone toward Rocco's medical bills.)

I try to see the whole ordeal (and it *was* an ordeal) as an unexpected bonus along my son's autism journey – because he (allegedly) ate a paint chip, we got to remodel part of our home, making the place safer and more comfortable for the whole family.

That's good, because our government loan ensures we'll be staying here for a *long* time...

EPILOGUE—WHAT'S THE WORST THING ABOUT BEING AUTISM DAD?

It's the look of sadness and pity I get from people. And, because I know people are coming from a sympathetic place (usually they're benefactors and/or people who love us) there's not a damn thing I can do about it.

The worst part about being Autism Dad is that people think it sucks. No one envies me. Nobody wants to be me.

People see my son, and they see the world of troubles he makes for my wife and I. They don't see what an awesome kid he is. They think, "Thank God he's not *my* kid."

Well, screw you, because I thank God every day that he's mine.

People are wrong. Being Autism Dad can be pretty damn awesome!

What changed between the dreary essays found earlier in this book and now?

I did.

My son's autism has made me a better parent and a better person. It's challenged me, pushed me to my limits and beyond, and freed me from an old way of thinking. It's helped me put a lot of things into perspective: I know what's important now, and what isn't.

Autism puts additional strain on a marriage, for sure, but it's also brought my wife and I closer in a lot of ways. We don't fight about petty stuff (and it seems that's what couples with "normal" kids always fight about). Having an autistic child has made us both wiser, more mature.

Every parent sees their child as "exceptional and unique," and, on some level, all children are. But my son, and other autistic children, are *truly* exceptional and unique. They don't experience the same world as the rest of us. They are one-of-a-kind...like puzzle pieces.

It's said that autistic children are like visitors from a foreign country, because they don't always understand the language and customs of our society. But sometimes I feel like my son is from another planet, or another realm of existence. Things look different to him, taste different, sound different, smell and feel different. Rather, his sensory input *means* something different to him than it does to you or I.

The term for this is Sensory Integration Disorder (SID), which is a big part of the autistic lifestyle. Temple Grandin, noted autistic spokesperson, author and doctor of animal science, liked being squeezed in a cattle press when she was young. Other kids like to spin, jump, flap hands, rock, etc. It's all part of orienting their bodies with their environment. Like I said, the world simply doesn't *feel* the same to them.

We went for a walk the other day, and Rocco was lagging behind. I kept urging him to catch up, until I realized what he was doing. One house had a stone wall around the property, and he was checking out the texture of each stone, rubbing his hands along the surface, moving his feet along the varying contours of the pavers, tracing their irregular shape, like a mini-mountain range.

I had the usual parental reaction: his hands were getting filthy, and the homeowner might not appreciate my son feeling up his wall. But I could almost understand Roc's desire to want to know *in detail* what those stones felt like. He probably would have rubbed his face against them, and taken a taste if I had let him. He had to *know*.

There are certainly downsides to my son's sensory needs (like eating soft soap...and lead paint chips). But some of Roc's sensory stims are enlightening. Watching golden sunlight dapple through the swaying limbs of a maple. The symmetrical shape water makes as it arcs from a sprinkler or garden hose, or when it breaks as a wave on the beach. The way a log tossed into fire will burn away from wood, to embers, to ash. These are but a few of the things I see differently now that I've seen them through my son's eyes. I don't know how I'll ever thank him.

Except maybe I do.

There are hard questions every Autism Dad must face: Will my child ever be able to live on his own? Will he be able to care for himself independently? Will he find friends? Love? What will happen to him when I'm gone?

These are the questions that haunt every Autism Dad. I certainly don't have any grand wisdom to offer here. It's scary stuff. Rocco's future is still uncertain; he's learned a lot, but he's still got a long way to go. One thing I'm sure of, though. He's a good kid, and he's growing into a fine man.

And if that man should need my day-to-day support for the rest of my life, I'd consider it an honor and a blessing. I love Rocco more than I've ever loved anyone, and living with him for the rest of my life would be far more of a hardship on *him* than it would me. He shows me how beautiful and wondrous the world can be, just by being in it.

Don't pity me. Being a caregiver—either of an autistic child or anyone else—means you have the chance every day to become a better human being by caring for another human being. It's taken me eight years (and those early days were *rough*), but I finally realized that being the father of an autistic child gives me a daily opportunity to be great. And, more often than not, I *am*.

I couldn't be more proud to be Rocco's Autism Dad!

About the Author

Rob Errera has worked as a writer, editor, musician, restaurant reviewer, restaurant manager, farm worker, factory janitor, convenience store clerk, and burger flipper. He is currently the Editor-in-Chief of CHERI Magazine and a columnist for Wayne Today, part of North Jersey Media Group. His fiction, non-fiction, and essays have earned numerous awards, including the First Annual Bloodcurdling Tales of Terror Contest. His work has appeared in *Starlog, New York Review of Science Fiction, Cinefantastique, Agony In Black, Wetbones, 2 A.M. Magazine*, and *Dark Recesses* among others. He lives in New Jersey with his wife, two kids, and a bunch of rescued dogs.

Roberrera.wordpress.com

Published by Giant Dog Books

Giantdog@earthlink.net

Made in the USA
Charleston, SC
20 February 2012